Francis Frith's
EXMOOR

PHOTOGRAPHIC MEMORIES

Francis Frith's
EXMOOR

◆

Dennis Needham

FRITH
BOOK Co

First published in the United Kingdom in 2000 by
Frith Book Company Ltd

Hardback Edition 2000
ISBN 1-85937-132-9

Paperback Edition 2002
ISBN 1-85937-608-8

British Library Cataloguing in Publication Data

Francis Frith's Exmoor
Dennis Needham

Frith Book Company Ltd
Frith's Barn, Teffont,
Salisbury, Wiltshire SP3 5QP
Tel: +44 (0) 1722 716 376
Email: info@francisfrith.co.uk
www.francisfrith.co.uk

Printed and bound in Great Britain

AS WITH ANY HISTORICAL DATABASE THE FRITH ARCHIVE IS CONSTANTLY BEING CORRECTED AND IMPROVED
AND THE PUBLISHERS WOULD WELCOME INFORMATION ON OMISSIONS OR INACCURACIES

Contents

◆

FRANCIS FRITH: *Victorian Pioneer*

FRANCIS FRITH, Victorian founder of the world-famous photographic archive, was a complex and fascinating man. A devout Quaker and a highly successful Victorian businessman, he was both philosophic by nature and pioneering in outlook.

By 1855 Francis Frith had already established a wholesale grocery business in Liverpool, and sold it for the astonishing sum of £200,000, which is the equivalent today of over £15,000,000. Now a multi-millionaire, he was able to indulge his passion for travel. As a child he had pored over travel books written by early explorers, and his fancy and imagination had been stirred by family holidays to the sublime mountain regions of Wales and Scotland. 'What a land of spirit-stirring and enriching scenes and places!' he had written. He was to return to these scenes of grandeur in later years to 'recapture the thousands of vivid and tender memories', but with a different purpose. Now in his thirties, and captivated by the new science of photography, Frith set out on a series of pioneering journeys to the Nile regions that occupied him from 1856 until 1860.

INTRIGUE AND ADVENTURE

He took with him on his travels a specially-designed wicker carriage that acted as both dark-room and sleeping chamber. These far-flung journeys were packed with intrigue and adventure. In his life story, written when he was sixty-three, Frith tells of being held captive by bandits, and of fighting 'an awful midnight battle to the very point of surrender with a deadly pack of hungry, wild dogs'. Sporting flowing Arab costume, Frith arrived at Akaba by camel seventy years before Lawrence, where he encountered 'desert princes and rival sheikhs, blazing with jewel-hilted swords'.

During these extraordinary adventures he was assiduously exploring the desert regions bordering the Nile and patiently recording the antiquities and peoples with his camera. He was the first photographer to venture beyond the sixth cataract. Africa was still the mysterious 'Dark Continent', and Stanley and Livingstone's historic meeting was a decade into the future. The conditions for picture taking confound belief. He laboured for hours in his wicker dark-room in the sweltering heat of the desert, while the volatile chemicals fizzed dangerously in their trays. Often he was forced to work in remote tombs and caves

where conditions were cooler. Back in London he exhibited his photographs and was 'rapturously cheered' by members of the Royal Society. His reputation as a photographer was made overnight. An eminent modern historian has likened their impact on the population of the time to that on our own generation of the first photographs taken on the surface of the moon.

VENTURE OF A LIFE-TIME

Characteristically, Frith quickly spotted the opportunity to create a new business as a specialist publisher of photographs. He lived in an era of immense and sometimes violent change. For the poor in the early part of Victoria's reign work was a drudge and the hours long, and people had precious little free time to enjoy themselves.

Most had no transport other than a cart or gig at their disposal, and had not travelled far beyond the boundaries of their own town or village. However, by the 1870s, the railways had threaded their way across the country, and Bank Holidays and half-day Saturdays had been made obligatory by Act of Parliament. All of a sudden the ordinary working man and his family were able to enjoy days out and see a little more of the world.

With characteristic business acumen, Francis Frith foresaw that these new tourists would enjoy having souvenirs to commemorate their days out. In 1860 he married Mary Ann Rosling and set out with the intention of photographing every city, town and village in Britain. For the next thirty years he travelled the country by train and by pony and trap, producing fine photographs of seaside resorts and beauty spots that were keenly bought by millions of Victorians. These prints were painstakingly pasted into family albums and pored over during the dark nights of winter, rekindling precious memories of summer excursions.

THE RISE OF FRITH & CO

Frith's studio was soon supplying retail shops all over the country. To meet the demand he gathered about him a small team of photographers, and published the work of independent artist-photographers of the calibre of Roger Fenton and Francis Bedford. In order to gain some understanding of the scale of Frith's business one only has to look at the catalogue issued by Frith & Co in 1886: it runs to some 670

pages, listing not only many thousands of views of the British Isles but also many photographs of most European countries, and China, Japan, the USA and Canada – note the sample page shown above from the hand-written *Frith & Co* ledgers detailing pictures taken. By 1890 Frith had created the greatest specialist photographic publishing company in the world, with over 2,000 outlets – more than the combined number that Boots and WH Smith have today! The picture on the right shows the *Frith & Co* display board at Ingleton in the Yorkshire Dales. Beautifully constructed with mahogany frame and gilt inserts, it could display up to a dozen local scenes.

POSTCARD BONANZA

◆ ◆

The ever-popular holiday postcard we know today took many years to develop. In 1870 the Post Office issued the first plain cards, with a pre-printed stamp on one face. In 1894 they allowed other publishers' cards to be sent through the mail with an attached adhesive halfpenny stamp. Demand grew rapidly, and in 1895 a new size of postcard was permitted called the

court card, but there was little room for illustration. In 1899, a year after Frith's death, a new card measuring 5.5 x 3.5 inches became the standard format, but it was not until 1902 that the divided back came into being, with address and message on one face and a full-size illustration on the other. *Frith & Co* were in the vanguard of postcard development, and Frith's sons Eustace and Cyril continued their father's monumental task, expanding the number of views offered to the public and recording more and more places in Britain, as the coasts and countryside were opened up to mass travel.

Francis Frith died in 1898 at his villa in Cannes, his great project still growing. The archive he created continued in business for another seventy years. By 1970 it contained over a third of a million pictures of 7,000 cities, towns and villages. The massive photographic record Frith has left to us stands as a living monument to a special and very remarkable man.

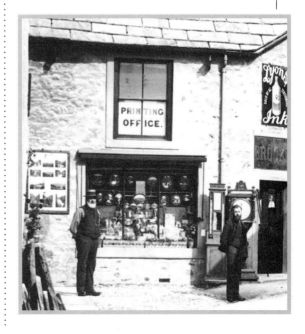

Frith's Archive: *A Unique Legacy*

FRANCIS FRITH'S legacy to us today is of immense significance and value, for the magnificent archive of evocative photographs he created provides a unique record of change in 7,000 cities, towns and villages throughout Britain over a century and more. Frith and his fellow studio photographers revisited locations many times down the years to update their views, compiling for us an enthralling and colourful pageant of British life and character.

We tend to think of Frith's sepia views of Britain as nostalgic, for most of us use them to conjure up memories of places in our own lives with which we have family associations. It often makes us forget that to Francis Frith they were records of daily life as it was actually being lived in the cities, towns and villages of his day. The Victorian age was one of great and often bewildering change for ordinary people, and though the pictures evoke an impression of slower times, life was as busy and hectic as it is today.

We are fortunate that Frith was a photographer of the people, dedicated to recording the minutiae of everyday life. For it is this sheer wealth of visual data, the painstaking chronicle of changes in dress, transport, street layouts, buildings, housing, engineering and landscape that captivates us so much today. His remarkable images offer us a powerful link with the past and with the lives of our ancestors.

TODAY'S TECHNOLOGY

Computers have now made it possible for Frith's many thousands of images to be accessed almost instantly. In the Frith archive today, each photograph is carefully 'digitised' then stored on a CD Rom. Frith archivists can locate a single photograph amongst thousands within seconds. Views can be catalogued and sorted under a variety of categories of place and content to the immediate benefit of researchers. Inexpensive reference prints can be created for them at the touch of a mouse button, and a wide range of books and other printed materials assembled and published for a wider, more general readership - in the next twelve months over a hundred Frith local history titles will be published! The

See Frith at www.francisfrith.co.uk

day-to-day workings of the archive are very different from how they were in Francis Frith's time: imagine the herculean task of sorting through eleven tons of glass negatives as Frith had to do to locate a particular sequence of pictures! Yet the archive still prides itself on maintaining the same high standards of excellence laid down by Francis Frith, including the painstaking cataloguing and indexing of every view.

It is curious to reflect on how the internet now allows researchers in America and elsewhere greater instant access to the archive than Frith himself ever enjoyed. Many thousands of individual views can be called up on screen within seconds on one of the Frith internet sites, enabling people living continents away to revisit the streets of their ancestral home town, or view places in Britain where they have enjoyed holidays. Many overseas researchers welcome the chance to view special theme selections, such as transport, sports, costume and ancient monuments.

We are certain that Francis Frith would have heartily approved of these modern developments, for he himself was always working at the very limits of Victorian photographic technology.

THE VALUE OF THE ARCHIVE TODAY

Because of the benefits brought by the computer, Frith's images are increasingly studied by social historians, by researchers into genealogy and ancestory, by architects, town planners, and by teachers and schoolchildren involved in local history projects. In addition, the archive offers every one of us a unique opportunity to examine the places where we and our families have lived and worked down the years. Immensely successful in Frith's own era, the archive is now, a century and more on, entering a new phase of popularity.

THE PAST IN TUNE WITH THE FUTURE

Historians consider the Francis Frith Collection to be of prime national importance. It is the only archive of its kind remaining in private ownership and has been valued at a million pounds. However, this figure is now rapidly increasing as digital technology enables more and more people around the world to enjoy its benefits.

Francis Frith's archive is now housed in an historic timber barn in the beautiful village of Teffont in Wiltshire. Its founder would not recognize the archive office as it is today. In place of the many thousands of dusty boxes containing glass plate negatives and an all-pervading odour of photographic chemicals, there are now ranks of computer screens. He would be amazed to watch his images travelling round the world at unimaginable speeds through network and internet lines.

The archive's future is both bright and exciting. Francis Frith, with his unshakeable belief in making photographs available to the greatest number of people, would undoubtedly approve of what is being done today with his lifetime's work. His photographs, depicting our shared past, are now bringing pleasure and enlightenment to millions around the world a century and more after his death.

EXMOOR – *An Introduction*

EXMOOR WAS A name to strike fear into the heart of travellers right into the 19th century. This was an area of bogs and crags, sparsely populated and virtually uncultivated. Roads were few, and most of the area's contact with the world beyond came via the sea through ports at Combe Martin and Lynmouth.

Man has lived on Exmoor for centuries. There is evidence of settlements right back to the stone age, but the moor discouraged even the Romans from detailed exploration; although they did visit, there was nothing like the colonisation that took place in other parts of the country.

Sporadic attempts at taming the Moor continued over the centuries, but it was not until the coming of the railways and the great boom in holidays that Exmoor was really opened up. The Great Western Railway built a line to Minehead and a route across the southern edge of the moor between Taunton and Barnstaple. This was not opened until 1873, a quarter of a century after the main railway developments further up-country.

But the north coast had to wait until 1898 before it saw the iron road. A narrow-gauge line was constructed between Barnstaple and Lynton, the scheme driven forward by the publisher Sir George Newnes, a Lynton resident. Unfortunately, there was little trade to sustain it, and by 1935 it was closed. But that short span of life was enough to awaken visitors' interest in both Lynton and the Moor. By this time, the motor car was becoming more popular, and with that popularity came the desire to explore. The remoteness that was the very essence of Exmoor was under threat as never before. Today, it is a place that can be easily visited and enjoyed. And visited it most certainly is: to hotels and farmhouse bed and breakfasts, to luxury caravan parks and small fields taking a couple of tents, visitors pour into and onto Exmoor.

By good fortune and, indeed, good planning, Exmoor itself is safe from major despoliation. In 1954, Parliament designated most of the Moor to be a National Park. At a mere 265 square miles, it is one of the smallest of our parks, but at least there is a statutory body responsible for the area. That it is frequently in conflict with residents of the Moor is almost par for the course. Planning and development are the usual areas of contention.

But politics aside, the Exmoor National Park is something rather special. Within its small boundaries you can discover an amazingly diverse collection of buildings, people and livestock. High hills - mountains almost - swoop down to become verdant valleys, and great rivers cleave their way through the rock, seeking the shortest passage to a salty tide. But one of the Moor's greatest rivers - the Exe - chooses a longer route. It rises high in the hills only a few miles from the Bristol Channel, but instead of heading that way, it flows south for 55 miles before emptying into the English Channel.

The East and West Lyn river combine at Lynmouth. Both follow exquisitely beautiful routes off the moor before arriving in the fishing village. But the charm and beauty visible today were distinctly absent in August 1952 when the village hit the headlines of the news media around the world. The rain had been pouring down on the Moor for over a day when the bands of a small dam burst. Water cascaded down, washing trees away as it went. These trees formed dams at successive bridges until the sheer weight of water caused each bridge to collapse and a wall of water careered down towards the next obstruction. The village was devastated, and 34 people lost their lives. Huge boulders were washed down, some so big that the army teams helping the clear-up needed explosives to shift them. Television was in its infancy then, but those with sets could experience the horror and drama at first hand as BBC cameramen visited the stricken village. Such views pumped into our homes had a major effect on the response of people up-country when help was needed.

One of the attractions of Exmoor is the ever-changing vistas as you travel along. Tiny villages with not much more than a pub are followed by a steep uphill section taking you away from cultivated land to high ground covered in heather and bracken, and boglands too. The weather on Exmoor is notoriously unreliable, and heavy rainfall can be expected at any time of the year.

Wildlife has always been a feature of

Lynmouth, The East and West Lyn 1911 63855

Exmoor life. The Exmoor Forest dates from Norman times, although it was never a forest as we understand the word. Then, the word was used to indicate an area for hunting: deer were the major quarry then, as now. Herds of wild deer still roam Exmoor, although their numbers are in a state of flux. The National Trust have banned hunting on their land, and

Not surprisingly, Exmoor has inspired some of our greatest poets. Robert Southey spent nine weeks during the summer of 1812 in Lynton. William Wordsworth lived with his sister Dorothy in the area, and often strayed to Exmoor in search of inspiration. He was friends with Samuel Taylor Coleridge, and the latter's 'Rime of the Ancient Mariner' was

Dunster, The Market and High Street 1919 69261

many of the staghounds now have limited territory in which to operate. Deer cause immense damage to crops and trees; farmers used to tolerate the deer whilst the hunt controlled them, but now they shoot on sight. Venison is plentiful, but the delicate balance between man and nature is currently well out of kilter. Wild ponies are still plentiful though. The Exmoor pony is a hardy breed, and will be found all over the Moor. Raptors are frequently seen as well; a kestrel hovering on the lookout for prey is a common sight. Slightly less so is the buzzard. They are most often seen high in the sky soaring along on thermals, or sitting on the top of wooden telephone poles, surveying the scene.

(according to Dorothy) planned on walks the three of them took in the direction of Lynton. The story has it that Coleridge wrote one of his greatest poems, 'Kubla Khan', under the influence of laudanum whilst living in a farmhouse near Porlock.

But perhaps the greatest literary figure of Exmoor is Richard Doddridge Blackmore. His novel 'Lorna Doone' is established as one of the great works of fiction. Scholars still argue as to what element of truth is contained in the story, but it seems likely that several of the characters were based on people who actually lived around the village of Malmsmead. Needless to say, the village has capitalised on this and there are Doone houses, churches and probably even tee-shirts.

But visitors to Exmoor a century ago were the exception rather than the norm. We can only be eternally grateful that one of them was Francis Frith. Probably carrying a cartload of equipment, he made his way around the area, picturing what he saw. And never forget that in those early days of photography, automatic focus, exposure, film loading and all the other gadgets we take for granted today were but a futuristic dream. Heavy wooden tripods, bulky cameras, glass plates - one for each view - and all the associated paraphernalia meant that travelling light was not an option. Each shot took an age to set up and execute. Subsequently, other cameramen employed by him returned to record the same views and thus allow us to follow the changes to both buildings and inhabitants.

What follows is a comprehensive record of life in one of England's more remote corners. Study the pictures, and note the way fashions developed. Absorb the dozens of small details that are revealed by the camera. Travel around in the footsteps of Francis Frith himself. Discover the locations he used, and stand on the very spot he chose. Take a photograph yourself, and then, at home, compare your view today with what he saw. The more you probe, the more you will realise that the pace of change has accelerated exponentially within the last forty years. Before that, Exmoor evolved gently rather than changed.

But whilst you may choose to relax in front of the fire with this volume, it really should inspire you to hit the road for Exmoor, to search out these locations and enjoy them anew. Exmoor is a friendly place to be enjoyed to the full. And, if these wonderful images of a gentler age thrill and delight you, do not forget to say thank you to Francis Frith for his foresight in capturing them for future generations.

Brayford, The Village c1955 B387003

DULVERTON
The Lion Hotel 1896 37653
This photograph shows an almost unchanged scene as far as the buildings are concerned. A century on, there are no coaches, no horses and the fashions have altered; but apart from the illuminated sign for The Lion hotel, the scene is identical today.

DULVERTON, FROM THE COTTAGE 1896 37652

Much of this scene can de identified today. The village has spread, and housing now covers the fields in the far centre and to the right. The river Barle runs through the town just before emptying into the Exe.

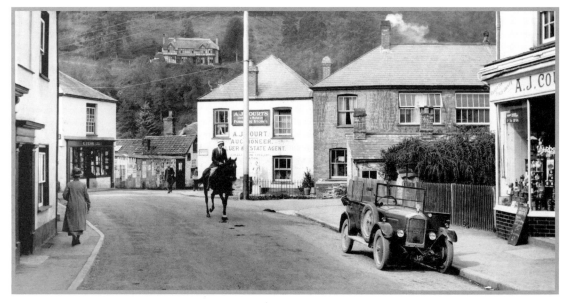

DULVERTON, HIGH STREET 1934 86312

The grocer's shop on the right still displayed the name 'A J Court' at the turn of this century. It is sad that it was no longer trading - doubtless the new owner will destroy this little bit of history. The large building to the right is Leat House, once a mill; the upstairs windows - designed to admit maximum light - have now been replaced by standard house-pattern ones. Court's Auctioneers is now a second-hand bookshop, and Venus (left) is now an antique dealers.

DULVERTON, ALL SAINTS CHURCH AND THE LYCHGATE 1934 86311

All Saints suffered a Victorian makeover; fortunately, the 13th-century tower was not ruined. The iron fence on the right has been moved to the other side of the path and the wall to the left removed, but otherwise there has been little change.

DULVERTON, THE BRIDGE 1886 19098

This view shows a peaceful scene as several boys perch precariously on the parapet watching a lone angler. Salmon and trout will be his quarry. To the left, one man and his dog relax. The barn across the water has now been rebuilt.

DULVERTON
Fore Street 1937 88173

Here we see another view of the town where little has changed. The butcher's on the left is now Gerald David & Sons, who sell 'home-killed meat from local farms'. Beyond the van, the first building to stand out is a post office. To the right, the cycle shop became a fishmonger's that has now closed.

EXMOOR, TARR STEPS 1929 82158

EXMOOR
Tarr Steps 1929

This famed packhorse bridge across the river Barle has been here for centuries. It is 180ft long with seventeen spans; some claim it was originally a Bronze Age crossing. The building in the background was a farm, but now serves excellent food and drink to the thousands of visitors to this popular and beautiful spot.

EXMOOR
Tarr Steps 1929

This view was taken from the opposite side to the photograph above. To the right, the river is quite shallow normally, so that wheeled vehicles and horses not happy on the slabs can ford the river. The Barle can flood violently, and the bridge was washed away in 1947, 1950 and 1980. The slabs are now numbered so that they can be retrieved and replaced in the correct order.

EXMOOR, TARR STEPS 1929 82159A

WINSFORD, THE ROYAL OAK 1930 83545
Rationalisation is the best way to describe the changes in this view today. The beautiful tree in the centre has gone, and a new building has been constructed near the signpost. The entrance to the Bar has been thatched in keeping with the rest of the pub, and the sign has been replaced.

WINSFORD, THE VILLAGE 1930 83547
Here we see an overview of the village, nestling as it does in the valley of the river Exe. The politician Ernest Bevin was born in Winsford in 1881. He became Foreign Secretary in the Attlee government of 1945.

WINSFORD, THE VILLAGE c1965 W112031

The village war memorial is on the right; the trees behind have been replaced. In front of the white cottage, the left-hand tree now dominates the view, whilst the white sign to the right indicates a ford.

WINSFORD, THE BLACKSMITH BRIDGE AND THE CHURCH c1965 W112027

This view shows one of the eight packhorse bridges in this tiny village. This one spans the river Winn. The church is dedicated to St. Mary, and is of Norman origin. Alterations and additions every century since make this a church of many architectural styles.

WINSFORD, THE BLACKSMITH BRIDGE AND THE ROYAL OAK HOTEL c1965 W112026

Here we see another view of the bridge, this time with the Royal Oak in the background. The thatched porch referred to in photograph No 83545 can be seen here. Apart from the man up a ladder, things do not change quickly in this corner of Exmoor.

WINSFORD, GENERAL VIEW c1965 W112030

Although dated less than fifty years ago, this view really is timeless. The horses, which in an earlier era would have been kept purely for work, now give pleasure to their owners. The 90ft tower of St. Mary is clear to see.

EXMOOR, THE CARACTACUS STONE c1960 E51017

EXMOOR
The Caractacus Stone c1960

Inscribed CARATACI NEPVS (descendant of Caractacus), this stone probably dates from the 6th century, although the letters are Roman, not Celtic. Caractacus was the chieftain of the Silures who fought - unsuccessfully - against the Roman invasion. Other authorities say that it is a standing stone from the Bronze Age - possibly a sacred stone marking the head of a stream - that was inscribed in situ.

◆

EXFORD
The Village 1892

This old photograph shows a venerable village. The left-hand building is now the Exmoor House Hotel; the shed in the centre is the hotel's car park and a garage is operating behind. A view of the 15th-century church of St. Mary is no longer possible from this spot - the trees have grown too tall.

EXFORD, THE VILLAGE 1892 31195

EXFORD
*The Village Centre
and the Bridge 1892* 31193

This view looks across to the White Horse Inn. The children are clearly fascinated by the photographer - possibly the first they had ever seen. The stone bridge over the Exe was originally of timber construction, as were most in the area. Some of these were not replaced until the 19th century.

EXFORD, THE VILLAGE 1940 89008

In the 42 years from photograph No 31193, the White Horse has been completely rebuilt. The tiles hanging on the left-hand wall have gone, and the surface is now rendered. Note the Ford and Rover cars - motoring is already starting to make its presence felt on the Moor.

EXFORD, THE VILLAGE 1940 89010

Behind the White Horse is a village green, and beyond that is the Crown Hotel. The hill in the centre carries is the main road heading east. The holly bush in the centre was planted to mark the coronation of King George V in 1911 and has grown to a prodigious size today.

EXFORD, THE CROWN HOTEL 1940 89009
Here we see the Crown from another angle. Note the top of an ancient fuel pump showing behind the nearest van. In the distance, a delivery van is attracting local ladies to buy its wares.

EXFORD, THE VILLAGE 1940 89011
This view was taken further up the street from the photograph above. The delivery van we saw then was parked outside the gabled building. To the right, the white building was Exford Post Office. Today, it is a private house with the downstairs door and shop window transposed. The post office - remarkably, still in business today - has moved next door with the 'Groceries and Provisions, Drapery and Hardware' - to say nothing of newspapers!

EXFORD, THE CROWN HOTEL c1955 E50020
Here we see a final view of the Crown taken fifteen years after the previous ones. The fuel pump is now plain to see, as are the old-fashioned oil dispensers. The foliage climbing the hotel's wall has now gone, along with the service station.

DUNSTER, THE OLD NUNNERY 1888 20919
This extraordinary building at the south end of the High Street is 14th-century, and was formerly known as The Chantry of St. Lawrence; it acted as a guest house for visitors to the priory. It acquired its present sobriquet around 1769.

DUNSTER, THE MARKET HOUSE 1890 27512
This photograph shows the High Street and the Yarn Market. This was built around 1589, indicating that the town was an important cloth-trading centre at that time. The turret on the hill is a folly, Conegar Tower, built around 1770. Up on the hill a century and a half ago, Mrs Cecil Frances Alexander sat. She composed the hymn 'All Things Bright and Beautiful' whilst admiring the view.

DUNSTER
The Market House and the Castle 1890 27511
Here we are looking along the High Street with Dunster
Castle in the distance. This was founded in 1070,
although much of the current building is 19th-century. It
was created by Anthony Salvin, who was also responsible
for Windsor Castle. He utilised many of the 17th- and
18th-century features of the castle in his rebuilding work.

DUNSTER

The Market and High Street 1919 69261

Little has changed in the thirty years since the previous photograph was taken. The Luttrell Arms on the left was originally the house of the abbot of Cleeve. The porch is medieval.

DUNSTER, WEST STREET 1897 40327

The large building to the left was a chapel when this picture was taken. Today, without the porch, it is Chapel House Crafts and Teas. The extreme right-hand building has become the Spears Cross Hotel.

DUNSTER, WEST STREET 1938 88721

As we look in the opposite direction to the photograph above, much has changed along the wide street. The New Inn is now the Stags Head, with the Exmoor House Hotel next door. The shop with the Hovis sign outside is particularly up-to-date: it is now the Internet Toy Shop.

DUNSTER, THE DOVECOT AND THE OLD PRIORY 1919 69262
St George's Church was originally part of the Benedictine Priory, which was founded in the 11th century. The church is some four hundred years younger. The round building is a dovecot: the monks kept up to 500 pigeons in here, which were killed for food during the winter months. It was restored in 1989.

DUNSTER, THE POLO GROUND 1927 80646
The main interest in this view is to look around the edge of the playing area. There are dozens of cars and a huge number of spectators - this was a time when cars were still a relative rarity.

CARHAMPTON, SEA LANE TO BLUE ANCHOR 1933 85931
This view is barely recognisable today with the main road directly behind the cameraman. The main building - Rose Cottage - has been extended, and the thatch has been replaced. The church and churchyard are behind the trees.

BLUE ANCHOR, THE BEACH 1935 87048
This view has disappeared, for erosion by the sea has washed away much of the outcrop. Behind the cars is a railway - a signal arm can just be seen. This is now effectively the edge of the sea; a sloping pebble beach now exists where the ladies are sitting beneath their parasols.

BLUE ANCHOR, THE RAILWAY 1935 87054

The railway here ran from Taunton to Minehead, and was a popular route for holidaymakers. All that notwithstanding, British Rail closed it on 2 January 1971. Fortunately, that was not the end of the story. A private company was formed immediately with the aim of re-opening it. This was (partially) achieved in 1976, when The West Somerset Railway started operating steam trains. Now the steam railway runs all the way from Minehead to the edge of Taunton at Bishops Lydeard. Behind the railway, the area is now a static caravan park.

BLUE ANCHOR, THE PROMENADE 1935 87052

We can see a more effective sea defence here at Blue Anchor. Only a few holidaymakers seem to be taking the bracing sea air, even though - to judge from the trees - it is high summer.

BLUE ANCHOR, THE VILLAGE 1936 87562
This is a similar view to photograph No 87052, but taken further to the east. On the right, the small farm building still exists, and a house has been built immediately behind the nearest telephone pole.

BLUE ANCHOR, THE SEA FRONT 1940 89002
Our photographer stood in the Blue Anchor pub to take this view of the village. Again, little has changed since those days, although the building in the foreground has acquired an extension to the left-hand end.

OLD CLEEVE, THE VILLAGE 1906 56810

Built on the lower slopes of a hill, this pretty and compact village looks generally westwards towards Minehead. To this day, there is much evidence of thatch to be seen. These particular buildings have even acquired thatched porches.

OLD CLEEVE, THE CHURCH AND THE COTTAGE 1930 83557

This view was taken a few yards to the right of the above photograph. The detached cottage is the same in both shots. Note that it has acquired a second chimney behind the existing one. The church is a fine Perpendicular-style building built from limestone.

OLD CLEEVE
The Pillared Cottage 1930 83556
Another view of this pretty village, again with thatch clearly
evident. The extension to the main building is supported
on two pillars - hence the name. Two youngsters are
intrigued by our cameraman, and a little further along the
road an aged perambulator lies in the gutter.

CLEEVE ABBEY, THE REFECTORY 1913 65347
This is part of the extensive ruins of Cleeve Abbey, one of the few 13th-century monastic sites where you can see such a complete set of buildings. When this photograph was taken, the ruin was in a state of disrepair.

CLEEVE ABBEY, THE ABBEY GATEWAY 1935 86615
Here we see the impressive gateway entrance to Cleeve Abbey. By 1950, some attempts were being made to preserve the structure. Today, its future is assured, as English Heritage is responsible for its upkeep. In 1998, the Abbey celebrated its 800th anniversary.

WASHFORD, THE VILLAGE 1913 65343

Today, the main road roars through Washford, but a few yards away you can find peace and seclusion, just as we see in this sequence of photographs taken before the days of the internal combustion engine. Here, the trees are no more, and a thatched garage now sits to the left, at the end of the first row of cottages. Then, apart from a decent road surface, the view is instantly recognisable.

WASHFORD, THE VILLAGE 1919 69282

Our cameraman is standing on a bridge over the Washford River to capture this view. The house to the right is now faced in stone and known (unsurprisingly) as Riverside Cottage. The white house at the end is now pink, and beyond it, but hidden from view, is the West Somerset Railway.

WASHFORD
The Village 1919 69281
This is the main road through Washford sweeping
round to the left. Today, the awkward bend is still
there, but the road is a little wider and smoother. The
signpost is no more, and the building behind it is
known as Walnut Tree Cottage.

WASHFORD, GENERAL VIEW 1930 83511

WASHFORD
General View 1930
A motorcycle and sidecar make their way through Washford. Note that the rider is without a helmet, an unusual sight in these safety-conscious times. The main road is now surfaced, and there are plenty of local businesses still operational. Today, hairdressing and bed and breakfast is all that is left.

◆

WASHFORD
The Village 1930
A final view of Washford reveals it as a rather small place. The West Somerset Railway is in the foreground - although at this time it was the Minehead branch of the Great Western Railway. In the bottom left-hand corner is an example of an extinct art: a thatched hay-rick, with a second one under construction alongside.

WASHFORD, THE VILLAGE 1930 83510

ROADWATER, THE VILLAGE 1930 83515

Further up the Washford river is the compact centre of Roadwater. Beyond this part, the place seems to go on for miles. This is strange, because the road from Washford arrives in the village, splits - and seems to go nowhere but into the hills. Only one narrow lane leads to anything other than a dead end.

ROADWATER, THE VILLAGE 1930 83517

As with so many villages hereabouts, thatch is the preferred roofing material. Many years ago, there was a railway through the village, which linked it to some iron ore workings further in the hills. That has been abandoned for a very long time. The Valiant Soldier Inn still serves a good pint of beer.

ALCOMBE, THE VILLAGE 1912 64872

Only cosmetic changes to this scene have been made after 90 years. The shop on the right is no more, but the white building to the left was at some stage converted to retailing and a large window was fitted to the left of the door. Now that has gone the way of so many of our small businesses, and is a private dwelling again.

ALCOMBE COMBE, THE VILLAGE 1930 83551

With the exception of the car, this view is completely unchanged. Alcombe was once a pretty little village, but the development from Minehead has seen its identity almost subsumed into the town. The A39 passing through the middle does not help much either.

MINEHEAD, THE PLUME OF FEATHERS 1892 31224
This view looks up Park Street away from The Parade. The central feature, the extended building with the fancy portico, is no more. Its replacement - a shop - is grotesque in the extreme. Note the gas street lighting, already installed.

MINEHEAD, THE PARADE 1903 49641
We are looking down the Parade from Wellington Square, again with the Plume of Feathers prominent. Even in those days, the establishment of retail outlets was taking place. Today it is the major shopping area for this end of Somerset. The nearest comparable town is Taunton, over twenty miles away.

MINEHEAD
The Parade 1903 49640
After exposing the previous photograph, our photographer
moved his camera a few yards further into The Parade to
capture this one. The ornate brick building started life as
the Market House: today, it is the Town Hall.

MINEHEAD
The Parade 1919 69249
It is sixteen years after the previous photograph and the camera is back again, this time further back in Park Street. A horse and cart wait in Wellington Square to the right, whilst alongside two policemen survey the apparently peaceful scene.

MINEHEAD, THE PARADE 1897 40333
This early view of The Parade looks towards Park Street. Note the small clock tower behind the trees. This must be one of the last views of this building because, as we shall see in the next photograph, it will be replaced.

MINEHEAD, THE PARADE 1903 49637
This grand building was completed in 1901. A new Market House was available to residents and holidaymaker alike. Next door, the more formal building with the elegant balustrade is a bank. Much of this corner of Minehead is devoted to Victorian development, whilst the old village, as we will soon see, is still relatively untouched.

MINEHEAD, THE PARADE 1927 80616

It is a few more years into the 20th century, and the motor car is now really making its presence felt. Nevertheless, horses are still clearly in use. The lighting standards that we saw earlier have now been replaced by something a little more ornate.

MINEHEAD, WELLINGTON SQUARE 1923 74993

There is a positive traffic jam in Wellington Square outside the Plume of Feathers. Compare this picture with photograph No 31224 and see how the ivy has covered the hotel wall in the passage of 31 years.

MINEHEAD, CHURCHDOWN 1888 20893
This view, with the cameraman's back to the church, is in Higher Town, the older part of Minehead. Standing in the same spot today, you will recognise it instantly. The path is a little more even, for the central section has been lined with blue engineers bricks. Otherwise, little has changed.

MINEHEAD, CHURCH STEPS 1903 49646
A century after this photograph was taken, only the ivy on the house to the right is no more. The church (St Michael's) continues to prosper. It is 15th-century, and has several treasures inside, including a 14th-century illuminated missal.

MINEHEAD, THE HARBOUR 1888 20888
This is a general view of the harbour, taken when much trade still reached the town by ship. Fishing boats were still active, as can be seen from this view. Many of the buildings to the right of centre were destroyed in 1897 when redevelopment took place.

MINEHEAD, THE QUAY 1897 40329
Here we see more shipping in the harbour at Minehead. Clearly, these small coastal sailing ships were still actively employed. Sail still ruled here at this time.

MINEHEAD, THE ESPLANADE 1901 47366

The buildings referred to in the 1888 view have now gone. A gasometer has appeared in the background, and sailing ships still rule the waters. Some of these vessels will now be ferrying coal across the Bristol Channel from South Wales to feed the gasworks.

MINEHEAD, THE QUAY 1919 69250

This view of the harbour shows only one vessel at anchor. On the extreme right is a shed-like object. This is a rail-mounted steam-powered crane, and would have been used to discharge coal and other cargoes from the boats.

MINEHEAD, THE HARBOUR 1927 80618
This is a wonderful evocative view of a harbour that belongs to a different era. Even the chain fence around the edge
has been replaced by a barrier constructed from scaffolding: the safety police are protecting us from ourselves again.

MINEHEAD, THE ESPLANADE 1903 49633
Holidaymakers are promenading along the Esplanade. The clothing is worthy of note: everyone wears a hat, for instance, and the little boy with the spade is togged out in a sailor suit - quite the fashion then.

MINEHEAD, THE ESPLANADE 1912 64866
Our cameraman is the centre of attraction again. Structurally, the Esplanade sea wall has been moved further out towards the beach. This allowed an extended road to be built to the extreme left of this view.

MINEHEAD, THE PROMENADE 1919 69237
Stone breakwaters on the right now protect the front from the might of the storms which sometimes batter this coast. The small shelter in the centre is still there and in use. Most of the housing to the left is substantially the same, but the shop fronts have acquired a somewhat tawdry appearance.

MINEHEAD, THE SANDS AND NORTH HILL 1923 74966
'Oh, I do like to be beside the sea-side ...' Minehead beach is clearly a popular place. But note that in both this and in the next photograph there is a preponderance of women. The date possibly gives a clue to the reason: it is only five years since the end of the Great War in which we lost virtually a generation of men.

MINEHEAD, THE STRAND PROMENADE 1923 74982
Cars are starting to make their presence felt now. The major change to this view is that there is now a succession of large stone and rubble breakwaters along the beach. The tent-like structure of Butlins now mars the skyline.

MINEHEAD, BUTLINS HOLIDAY CAMP c1960 M84236
At this time, a family holiday at Butlins was a popular option. Special trains ran from all over the country bringing in thousands intent on a jolly good time. Many camps had their own private station where visitors could step from the train into reception, find their chalet, turn the children loose and relax.

MINEHEAD, BUTLINS HOLIDAY CAMP c1960 M84253
Although in a much altered form, the holiday camp still exists. Back in their heyday, they were also popular with teenagers, who used to book as single sex parties, but would team up with the opposite sex pretty quickly after arrival. Many romances (and forced marriages in those more Puritan times) resulted from a week at Butlins.

MINEHEAD
The Old Town 1890

This is a view of the old buildings directly behind the harbour. The ones to the right have gone, and a road exists in their place. The first major building on the left is now rebuilt as The Red Lion pub.

MINEHEAD 1903

This atmospheric photograph shows Greenaleigh Farm, which is on the lower slope of North Hill to the west of the town. It truly captures life as it was a century ago: ankle-length dresses, an unsurfaced road and chickens foraging in what we would today call free-range conditions.

MINEHEAD, THE OLD TOWN 1890 27505

MINEHEAD 1903 50471

SELWORTHY, THE VILLAGE 1883 15836

This is another beautiful corner in this area which has so many. Although captioned as Selworthy, the actual location of this delightful building (and a replacement tree) is just off the main road in an area known as Holnicote.

SELWORTHY, DAME'S COTTAGE c1871 5994

The centre of this gorgeous village is now owned by the National Trust. This will ensure that the seven old houses around a village green will remain unchanged. Their deep thatch, latticed windows and lush surroundings are quite exquisite.

SELWORTHY, THE ALMSHOUSES 1900 45701

These delightful houses were built in the mid 19th century by Sir Thomas Dyke Acland for pensioners. Much of the Acland land was given to the National Trust in 1944 by his great-great-grandson Sir Richard Acland. He believed in public ownership on moral grounds, and formed the Common Wealth Party with the author J B Priestley in 1942.

LUCCOMBE, THE COTTAGES 1890 23527

If the Luccombe of this photograph is not instantly recognisable, the rest of the village continues to offer thatch by the acre. The Acland/National Trust connection is the same here as it is in Selworthy.

EXMOOR, THE SUMMIT, DUNKERY BEACON c1960 E51042

EXMOOR
The Summit, Dunkery Beacon c1960

Over 1700ft above sea level, this is the highest point on Exmoor. The nearest road is well over half a mile away, so the only way to get here is on foot. On a really clear day, the views are spectacular: you can see the Brecon Beacons in Wales to the north, Dartmoor to the south and the Mendips to the east.

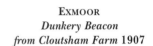

EXMOOR
Dunkery Beacon from Cloutsham Farm 1907

This view of Dunkery looks over the thickly wooded valley of East Water. Note the lady to the left tending her hens. This was back in the days when poultry ran free on every farm.

EXMOOR, DUNKERY BEACON FROM CLOUTSHAM FARM 1907 58379

HORNER
Horner Mill 1890

The miller and his dog are no more, but otherwise most of this scene survives. The large tree is now a stump, and a stone wall guards the property which is set in sylvan surroundings just above Horner.

◆

ALLERFORD
Corner of the Village 1923

The carefully-posed urchins add a nice extra dimension to an otherwise rather bland view. The road is the main A39, which swerves to avoid the village of Allerford, a most charming place. The building is now Cross Lane House, a licensed hotel and restaurant.

HORNER, HORNER MILL 1890 23532

ALLERFORD, CORNER OF THE VILLAGE 1923 75023

ALLERFORD, THE BRIDGE 1890 23519

The two-arched packhorse bridge is but one of the attractions in Allerford. The building to the right has gone, replaced by 'The Packhorse Holiday Flats'; the most interesting building is the thatched one beyond the bridge. It looks quite shabby and run-down.

ALLERFORD, THE BRIDGE 1900 45704

But a decade after photograph No 23519, the thatched building has had a makeover. Tiles replace the thatch, the chimneys have a basic cowling system and window frames have been replaced. A century along, it is still smart and has acquired the name of Packhorse Cottage. Someone must have thought long and hard to come up with that name!

ALLERFORD, THE VILLAGE 1923 75021

This is a general view of the village, taken a little further along the road from the bridge. Horses are still in use, and the road surface leaves something to be desired.

ALLERFORD, THE VILLAGE 1923 75024

After taking the above photograph, our photographer moved beyond where the horses were for this view of the two ladies riding off. He must have been standing alongside the motorcycle combination. Was this his transport? Did he arrive in Allerford, see the horses and quickly dismount for the photograph?

ALLERFORD
Piles Mill 1931
Across the A39, this is another building
in the care of the National Trust. No
water flows along the leat today, and the
ivy has been cleared from the building,
leaving it a little more recognisable.

BOSSINGTON
The Village 1931
A large new chimney is the only real
change to this splendid view. Again, note
the poor road surface - more than ade-
quate for the only traffic that appears in
this view, but recent rain has left several
puddles.

ALLERFORD, PILES MILL 1931 84856

BOSSINGTON, THE VILLAGE 1931 84861

BOSSINGTON, THE FAMOUS WALNUT TREE c1950 B154001

The famous walnut tree is no more. Having become dangerous, it was felled, but a new one of the same variety has been planted. Maybe in a couple of centuries visitors to Bossington will see something resembling this view again. Another example of stunning originality can be found in the name of the building: Walnut Tree Cottage.

BOSSINGTON, THE VILLAGE c1955 B154005

Bossington is really nothing more than a dead end, a cluster of houses alongside Horner Water just before it reaches the pebbly beach in Porlock Bay. This remoteness is, in part, what makes it so attractive.

BOSSINGTON, THE VILLAGE AND BOSSINGTON FARM c1955 B154007

The narrow streets are completely unsuitable for cars. Nevertheless, they visit to this day, although a small car park is now provided alongside the river. Note the incidence of tall chimneys here: they are probably necessary with Porlock Vale to the west, the direction of the prevailing wind here, and Bossington Hill and Selworthy Beacon downwind - the latter rears up to 1,000 feet above sea level.

PORLOCK, THE SHIP INN 1890 23509

This view really belongs to another age: we see horse transport, narrow streets and carefully-posed people and animals. The Ship is still in business; apart from the removal of the two porches, it is substantially unchanged.

PORLOCK, HIGH STREET 1890 23512

The Castle Inn seems to be drawing good trade, as it does now. The building we see was destroyed by fire many years ago and rebuilt. Across the way, the ivy has been removed to reveal an attractive cottage offering accommodation to visitors, of which there are many.

PORLOCK, DOVERHAY 1919 69272

More tall chimneys are in evidence in Porlock. Again, plenty of thatch helps to create a timeless English scene, one that is becoming increasingly rare. There are several piles of horse manure on the road surface.

PORLOCK

High Street 1919 69270

Mr. Burgess the baker is no more, and so is his horse and cart, which delivered fresh crusty bread (without hygienic wrappings to destroy the crustiness) around the village. Today, his premises retail gifts for visitors. Across the way, in a reversal of the norm, the tiled roof has been thatched, and the shop is now a bed and breakfast.

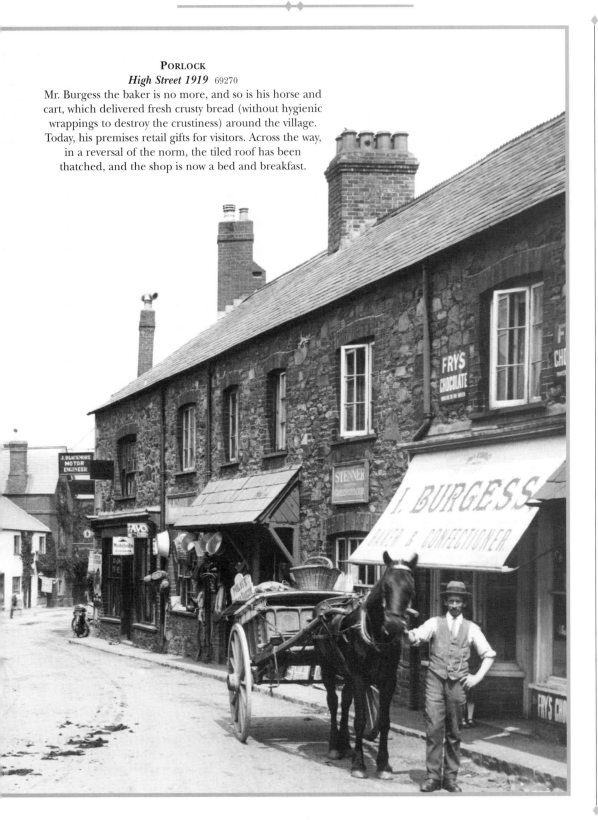

PORLOCK, HIGH STREET 1927 80628
Now, the motor has invaded Porlock. Then, as today, the narrow streets make it a difficult place to drive through. Again, the road surface seems relatively neglected, although the pavement appears to be in good repair.

PORLOCK, THE DEVON AND SOMERSET STAGHOUNDS 1907 58573c
The crowds, both on horseback and on foot, indicate the popularity of hunting in these parts both then and to this day. Both this and fox-hunting is still considered locally as the only effective way of controlling vermin. This way of life is increasingly under threat by anti-hunting campaigners. The D & S - as it is known - continues to draw huge support; shows, point to point and hunt balls continue to be an integral part of the social fabric of Exmoor.

EXMOOR, EXMOOR PONIES C1960 E51053

Exmoor ponies are no longer a true 'wild' breed, although they roam freely all over the Moor. Bigger than a Shetland, standing usually at around thirteen hands, their thick coats are well-suited to the rigours of life up in the hills. They are also a vital part of the ecosystem, dining on gorse, heather and bracken that would otherwise swamp the Moor.

EXMOOR, EXMOOR SHEEP C1965 E51062

The Exmoor Horn sheep are a breed developed to withstand the sometimes harsh weather on Exmoor. Today, they are not so common, having been cross-bred with other breeds to produce the sort of meat the supermarkets tell us we like today. How long sheep-farming on Exmoor will survive, given the Common Agricultural Policy, will remain to be seen. Without stock grazing, the Moor will become unrecognisable very quickly.

EXMOOR, THE RIVER LYN c1965 E51064
The East Lyn, high up on the moor at Robbers Bridge, is a popular place for cars to visit today. Children play by the waterside whilst their parents picnic. Some of the rustic charm may have been lost, but the beauty remains.

EXMOOR, THE DOONE VALLEY c1960 E51001
The Doone story is almost certainly fiction. But there was a band of robbers and freebooters active here two centuries before Blackmore knew the area. He skilfully wove together tales of these villains, which he probably heard in his childhood, with actual locations that he knew. This is what makes the tale so convincing.

MALMSMEAD, LORNA DOONE'S FARM c1960 M14301

Needless to say, the tourism industry, having got hold of the story, exploited it to the full. Lorna Doone's this, that and the other are to be found in and around Malmsmead and up the Badgworthy valley. This pretty scene is in Malmsmead. The narrow bridge is an alternative to the ford, just to the right of it.

EXMOOR, THE BADGWORTHY VALLEY c1874 7260

The valley of Badgworthy Water, which joins the East Lyn river at Malmsmead, is now universally known as Doone Country: even the Ordnance Survey have adopted the name. The river rises high on Exmoor, and for much of its length forms the county line between Devon and Somerset.

BRENDON, THE STAG HUNTERS INN C1965 B194030
Nestling in the East Lyn valley, Brendon is handsome and rugged, compared with the villages in the Porlock area which may be described as pretty. This view of The Stag Hunters Inn remains the same today, except that the chance of seeing an early post-war Ford outside is pretty remote now.

BRENDON, THE VILLAGE 1911 63861
An indication of the way Brendon sits in the valley can be gained from this view. The housing stock is altogether more sturdy - it has to withstand the harshness of the winters up here.

BRENDON, FROM THE WEST 1911 63862

The rolling slopes of Exmoor are clearly illustrated here. On the left, Brendon Common is a wild area of pure Exmoor where the land reaches 1300ft above sea level.

ROCKFORD, THE VILLAGE c1960 B194020

Rockford stands a mile further downstream from Brendon. The 17th-century Rockford Inn on the left still sells cider, but it is not advertised on the wall in such a delightful way as it was when this view was taken. The photograph was taken halfway across a footbridge over the East Lyn river.

COUNTISBURY, THE BLUE BALL INN 1907 59405
The postman stands outside the Blue Ball Inn, high up on Countisbury Hill. This track is now the main A39 road, and is somewhat wider than it was when this view was taken.

COUNTISBURY, THE BLUE BALL INN 1907 59406
After the postman had gone (see the above photograph) the Lynton to Porlock coach arrived. Note the extra horses on the front, complete with postillion. The coach has just ascended a hill with grades of up to 1 in 4, the reason for the extra horsepower. This service lasted until 1913.

COUNTISBURY, THE BLUE BALL INN 1929 82248

Twenty years after the previous two photographs, the road is starting to be improved. The open-topped coach is owned by Southdown Moors, based in Sussex, an immense journey in those days. At the end of the last century, The Blue Ball succumbed to the latest fashion of re-naming pubs which have remained unchanged for centuries. Today, expect to take a pint at the Exmoor Sandpiper.

COUNTISBURY, THE CHURCH 1907 59407

High on the top of Countisbury Hill stands the church of St John the Evangelist. There is little of interest inside the building, but note the squat tower: it offers not too much resistance to the winds that howl along this section of coast.

COUNTISBURY, THE LIGHTHOUSE 1911 63875
The finger of land pointing northwards into the Bristol Channel at Countisbury is known as Foreland Point. The lighthouse here warns shipping of the potential disaster on these sheer cliffs. Today, there is no keeper; it is operated automatically.

LYNMOUTH
The East and West Lyn 1911

This scene is no more. After the 1952 tragedy, the confluence of the rivers was altered to reduce the chance of a repetition to a minimum. Along with the changed river course, the buildings have also been swept away.

LYNMOUTH
The Pier and the Rhenish Tower 1899

The Rhenish Tower, built by a General Rawdon to store seawater for bathing, was destroyed in the flood. A replacement has been built, and the quay has been extended a little beyond what is seen here. The posts in the sea beyond mark the channel for boats entering or leaving harbour. The buildings to the left survived the tempest and look similar today.

LYNMOUTH, THE EAST AND WEST LYN 1911   63855

LYNMOUTH, THE PIER AND THE RHENISH TOWER 1899   43095

LYNMOUTH
The Village c1930 L126301
Although the 20th century was well under way when this view was taken, the use of sail is still quite apparent. The building to the left, Rock House, still exists; the one right on top of the cliff has gone. The second building on the right is the lifeboat station.

LYNMOUTH
Cherry Bridge 1907
Thatched cottages, sheep dogs and a babe-in-arms conjure up images of an earlier, more peaceful age. Certainly, with the amount of traffic around here now, this scene could not be repeated.

LYNTON
View over the Roofs c1965
Note that the housing ends suddenly as the sheer cliffs plunge down to the sea and the village of Lynmouth below. The building towards the left rear with flag-poles is the town hall.

LYNMOUTH, CHERRY BRIDGE 1907 59424

LYNTON, VIEW OVER THE ROOFS c1965 L127074

LYNTON, THE CHURCH c1965 L27073

The church in Lynton is built of grey stone, a feature shared with many other buildings in town. This makes the whole place look a little dowdy; this does not match the character of the town, which is cheerful and thriving.

LYNTON, NORTH WALK 1908 61100

The steeply sloping cliff face below Lynton offers some scope for paths cut into the side, as well as some housing and a hotel or two. Here a couple are enjoying a gentle perambulation. Beyond them, a path leads around the base of Hollerday Hill into the Valley of the Rocks, one of the area's best-known features.

LYNTON, THE VALLEY OF THE ROCKS HOTEL 1907 59372
A coach is ready to leave the hotel. Judging by the number of people on top, it must have been quite an unstable ride. By this time, the narrow-gauge railway from Barnstaple had reached Lynton. The most likely destination would have been Porlock. Note the uniformed character by the door, posing with his horn ready to blow.

BARBROOK, BEGGARS ROOST 1935 86632

This is the West Lyn river valley. To the left, opposite a road junction, is a post office; behind, but completely buried in the trees, is the Lynton to Barnstaple railway. The Porlock road sweeps in from the right to the post office: turn right to Lynton, left to Barnstaple. In more recent times, the junction has moved, with the building of a new section of road alongside the houses immediately below.

BARBROOK, THE VILLAGE 1935 86631

The location of the new road mentioned in the above photograph can be more easily seen in this view. Where the road currently turns left, the link runs in front of the white house to join the existing road behind the trees. The small building opposite the white house is St Bartholomew's church.

PARRACOMBE, THE VILLAGE 1907 59422

The church to the right is Christ Church, built in 1878 to replace St Petrock's. The pub to the left was quite new when this view was taken. There has been a public house on this site for centuries, but a major fire at the end of the 19th century destroyed the previous (thatched) building.

PARRACOMBE, FROM FAIRFIELD 1907 59438

Our photographer climbed the hill for this view. The street to the left is where he took the above photograph, and the end-on building is the pub. This view shows the way that Parracombe nestles in its little valley.

PARRACOMBE, FROM CASTLE HILL 1907 59439
The 'castle' referred to in the title was Holwell Castle, a medieval motte and bailey construction. There has been some development in the village since this view was captured, and housing can now be seen all around the church.

PARRACOMBE, THE OLD CHURCH OF ST PETROCK 1907 59443
In 1969, a Pastoral Measure (a church law carrying the same status as an Act of Parliament) was passed to preserve special churches that were no longer required for worship. St Petrock's was the very first one selected. Because there were doubts about its stability and a new church had been built, St Petrock's escaped the depredations of the Victorian restorers; it has thus retained its 17th-century interior, a very rare survival.

PARRACOMBE, THE CHURCH AND THE SCHOOL c1955 P11003
Here we have a closer look at St Petrock's replacement building, which is much closer to the village. The stone building to the left of the church is the Police station. It was later converted into flats and renamed Peel House.

PARRACOMBE, THE FOX AND GOOSE HOTEL c1960 P11056
This is the main street through the village, with the Fox and Goose on the right. To the left, behind the tractor, is the pub's car park, and the river Hedon flows from left to right. On the tractor, the driver looks asleep or drunk - or both?

COMBE MARTIN, THE HARBOUR 1926 79238

Four youngsters playing on a beached rowing boat is a scene repeated through history. Their parents (perhaps) are sitting on the next boat, watching the comings and goings of this tiny harbour area. Note the lobster pot alongside, and the huge ropes and chains used for securing visiting ships.

COMBE MARTIN
View from Above 1930 83464
The beach in the foreground where the boats are moored is made of
shingle. A more sandy beach can be found beyond the rocky promon-
tory. The road heading away on the right leads to Ilfracombe, and the
western end of the Exmoor hills can be seen to the left.

COMBE MARTIN, A SCHOONER IN THE HARBOUR 1935 86745
A schooner is tied up in what passes for Combe Martin harbour. In reality, it is little more than a natural inlet. It is strange to realise that as recently as 1935, sail was still in use in this area. The hill to the right is Lester Cliff, which offers an excellent view over the harbour.

COMBE MARTIN, NEWBERRY BEACH AND THE PARADE 1934 86439
Here we see a host of visitors enjoying the mild Devon climate. Deck-chairs are still a major feature of seaside life at this time; the more esoteric varieties we use today are still well into the future.

COMBE MARTIN, THE HARBOUR AND THE ESPLANADE 1911 63962
This is an early view of the village, with a couple posing self-consciously. The Ilfracombe road curves away in the
distance, whilst the river Hedon arrives at the sea in the centre of this view close to the retaining wall.

COMBE MARTIN, SEASIDE HILL 1930 83456

ARLINGTON, THE POST OFFICE c1960 A146014

COMBE MARTIN
Seaside Hill 1930
Visitors are strolling around the lower end of the village. Combe Martin is a long and straggling, clinging to either side of the narrow combe for well over a mile inland. This restful scene was once quite an industrial one. Both lead and silver were mined a short distance inland, and the ore was shipped across to South Wales for processing.

ARLINGTON
The Post Office c1960
The estate village of Arlington with its old post office - now Mill Cottages - lies alongside the Lynton to Barnstaple road. Arlington Court, behind and to the left, was owned by the Chichester family from the 13th century until 1947, when the last surviving family member gave it to the National Trust. The first round-the-world solo yachtsman Sir Francis Chichester was a member of the family and is buried in north Devon.

BRATTON FLEMING, THE VILLAGE STREET c1955 B383003

This is a typical village of the western edge of Exmoor, although outside the National Park. Bratton Fleming is essentially a few houses straggling along either side of a road on a hillside. In this view, the village post office (the low-roofed white-painted building in the centre) still manages to survive. The larger building beyond the car is a Baptist church.

BRATTON FLEMING, THE WHITE HART HOTEL c1955 B383002

The centre of life in Bratton Fleming, the White Hart has changed over the years. Extended, and with an upper storey added to the building on the right, the pub is now a free house; Starkey's ales are but a fond memory.

BRATTON FLEMING, THE CHURCH c1955 B383001
St Peters is of limited interest, for it was one of those 'improved' by our Victorian ancestors. Their version of improvement would not gain much currency today. The clock in the tower was installed in 1897.

BRATTON FLEMING, THE VILLAGE STREET c1955 B383005
The buildings on the extreme left - including the National Benzole sign - have made way for an altogether more modern garage. Butlers fuels are now on offer. This is located across the road from the White Hart.

BRAYFORD, FROM CHARLES HILL c1955 B387001

This photograph gives a pleasant overview of the village, which just about sneaks into the definition of 'Exmoor' it is on the outer fringes to the west. It certainly has all the qualities of a Moor village, and the hills in the distance are Exmoor proper.

BRAYFORD, THE POST OFFICE c1955 B387004

This view is absolutely timeless. The phone box is now red, a wall replaces the railings on the bridge, and the furthest building has acquired an extra storey. Otherwise, there has been no change.

BRAYFORD, THE VILLAGE c1955 B387003
This view is what the visitor sees as he drops down into the village from the main road. Little change has taken place over the years, apart from the loss of the building behind the Leyland lorry. The large building in the middle distance is the Methodist church.

HEASLEY HILL, THE VILLAGE c1955 H238015

This is a charming hamlet, set in the valley of the river Mole. It is hard to believe that in such an apparently peaceful area, mining took place up the valley. Iron and copper were worked, and lead, tin and even silver were found in smaller quantities. Once, a tramway ran through here carrying ore to the railway at South Molton.

HEASLEY HILL, THE VILLAGE c1955 H238013

The photographer has now moved to the south of Heasley Hill to capture much more of an Exmoor view. Again, the Mole valley disappears north into the trees, not far from its source. The white house can now be seen in a little more detail.

HEASLEY HILL, HEASLEY HOUSE c1955 H238019

The white building is a delightful country hotel, The Heasley House Hotel. This is a most charming establishment, and ever-popular with visitors. Note that the house next door has a set of stags' antlers over the door. This is a regular adornment of buildings on Exmoor. It does not denote a dead beast; deer shed their antlers every year and grow a new set.

HEASLEY HILL
The Green c1955

The photographer stood with his back to the hotel to capture this view. The left-hand building has acquired a slate roof, and the right-hand barn is now a house. Note the old plough alongside the road sign.

NORTH MOLTON
The Old Bridge c1955

The sides of the parapet have been replaced with an outward-leaning wire fence following regular contact between motor vehicle and stone. Otherwise, this pretty scene is essentially unchanged.

HEASLEY HILL, THE GREEN c1955 H238020

NORTH MOLTON, THE OLD BRIDGE c1955 N60020

NORTH MOLTON, THE VILLAGE c1955 N60001

North Molton tends to be something of a plain village, as the houses here show. It once flourished in the time of the wool trade; then mining became the main source of wealth. There is still a Miners Arms pub in town.

NORTH MOLTON, THE SQUARE c1955 N60018

Tom Faggus was the local blacksmith who had his smithy here in the Square. A gentleman of that name appears in the Lorna Doone story, and Faggus was a highwayman at one stage of his life. Exmoor was a wild place in years gone by: with highwaymen, bands of robbers, the weather and, later, hordes of drunken miners, the Moor was a place to avoid. The vehicle in the picture is a Morris Minor van.

NORTH MOLTON, GENERAL VIEW 1900 6319
All Saints church dominates this distant view of North Molton. The perpendicular tower has since lost the small turrets on the very top.

NORTH MOLTON, THE VILLAGE c1955 N60002
This distant view of the village shows quite clearly that compared with some of the villages visited by the photographers, North Molton comes a poor second in the beauty stakes.

SIMONSBATH, THE CAIRN c1960 S131003

SIMONSBATH
The Cairn c1960

This cairn, alongside a minor road to the south-west of Simonsbath, commemorates Sir John William Fortescue, historian of the British Army, 1859–1933. He was born in Madeira, and was librarian at Windsor Castle between 1905 and 1926. His 13-volume 'History of the British Army 1899-1930' is the definitive work on the subject.

◆

SIMONSBATH
The Exmoor Forest Hotel 1907

The sign on the left indicates that at the time this photograph was taken, this was a temperance hotel. Much has changed since then. The fence has gone, and a car park has been constructed. The road to the right has been surfaced, but the main structure of the building remains.

SIMONSBATH, THE EXMOOR FOREST HOTEL 1907 59434

Index

Frith Book Co Titles

www.francisfrith.co.uk

The Frith Book Company publishes over 100 new titles each year. A selection of those currently available are listed below. For latest catalogue please contact Frith Book Co.

Town Books 96 pages, approx 100 photos. County and Themed Books 128 pages, approx 150 photos (unless specified). All titles hardback laminated case and jacket except those indicated pb (paperback)

Title	ISBN	Price	Title	ISBN	Price
Amersham, Chesham & Rickmansworth (pb)	1-85937-340-2	£9.99	Derby (pb)	1-85937-367-4	£9.99
			Derbyshire (pb)	1-85937-196-5	£9.99
Ancient Monuments & Stone Circles	1-85937-143-4	£17.99	Devon (pb)	1-85937-297-x	£9.99
Aylesbury (pb)	1-85937-227-9	£9.99	Dorset (pb)	1-85937-269-4	£9.99
Bakewell	1-85937-113-2	£12.99	Dorset Churches	1-85937-172-8	£17.99
Barnstaple (pb)	1-85937-300-3	£9.99	Dorset Coast (pb)	1-85937-299-6	£9.99
Bath (pb)	1-85937419-0	£9.99	Dorset Living Memories	1-85937-210-4	£14.99
Bedford (pb)	1-85937-205-8	£9.99	Down the Severn	1-85937-118-3	£14.99
Berkshire (pb)	1-85937-191-4	£9.99	Down the Thames (pb)	1-85937-278-3	£9.99
Berkshire Churches	1-85937-170-1	£17.99	Down the Trent	1-85937-311-9	£14.99
Blackpool (pb)	1-85937-382-8	£9.99	Dublin (pb)	1-85937-231-7	£9.99
Bognor Regis (pb)	1-85937-431-x	£9.99	East Anglia (pb)	1-85937-265-1	£9.99
Bournemouth	1-85937-067-5	£12.99	East London	1-85937-080-2	£14.99
Bradford (pb)	1-85937-204-x	£9.99	East Sussex	1-85937-130-2	£14.99
Brighton & Hove(pb)	1-85937-192-2	£8.99	Eastbourne	1-85937-061-6	£12.99
Bristol (pb)	1-85937-264-3	£9.99	Edinburgh (pb)	1-85937-193-0	£8.99
British Life A Century Ago (pb)	1-85937-213-9	£9.99	England in the 1880s	1-85937-331-3	£17.99
Buckinghamshire (pb)	1-85937-200-7	£9.99	English Castles (pb)	1-85937-434-4	£9.99
Camberley (pb)	1-85937-222-8	£9.99	English Country Houses	1-85937-161-2	£17.99
Cambridge (pb)	1-85937-422-0	£9.99	Essex (pb)	1-85937-270-8	£9.99
Cambridgeshire (pb)	1-85937-420-4	£9.99	Exeter	1-85937-126-4	£12.99
Canals & Waterways (pb)	1-85937-291-0	£9.99	Exmoor	1-85937-132-9	£14.99
Canterbury Cathedral (pb)	1-85937-179-5	£9.99	Falmouth	1-85937-066-7	£12.99
Cardiff (pb)	1-85937-093-4	£9.99	Folkestone (pb)	1-85937-124-8	£9.99
Carmarthenshire	1-85937-216-3	£14.99	Glasgow (pb)	1-85937-190-6	£9.99
Chelmsford (pb)	1-85937-310-0	£9.99	Gloucestershire	1-85937-102-7	£14.99
Cheltenham (pb)	1-85937-095-0	£9.99	Great Yarmouth (pb)	1-85937-426-3	£9.99
Cheshire (pb)	1-85937-271-6	£9.99	Greater Manchester (pb)	1-85937-266-x	£9.99
Chester	1-85937-090-x	£12.99	Guildford (pb)	1-85937-410-7	£9.99
Chesterfield	1-85937-378-x	£9.99	Hampshire (pb)	1-85937-279-1	£9.99
Chichester (pb)	1-85937-228-7	£9.99	Hampshire Churches (pb)	1-85937-207-4	£9.99
Colchester (pb)	1-85937-188-4	£8.99	Harrogate	1-85937-423-9	£9.99
Cornish Coast	1-85937-163-9	£14.99	Hastings & Bexhill (pb)	1-85937-131-0	£9.99
Cornwall (pb)	1-85937-229-5	£9.99	Heart of Lancashire (pb)	1-85937-197-3	£9.99
Cornwall Living Memories	1-85937-248-1	£14.99	Helston (pb)	1-85937-214-7	£9.99
Cotswolds (pb)	1-85937-230-9	£9.99	Hereford (pb)	1-85937-175-2	£9.99
Cotswolds Living Memories	1-85937-255-4	£14.99	Herefordshire	1-85937-174-4	£14.99
County Durham	1-85937-123-x	£14.99	Hertfordshire (pb)	1-85937-247-3	£9.99
Croydon Living Memories	1-85937-162-0	£9.99	Horsham (pb)	1-85937-432-8	£9.99
Cumbria	1-85937-101-9	£14.99	Humberside	1-85937-215-5	£14.99
Dartmoor	1-85937-145-0	£14.99	Hythe, Romney Marsh & Ashford	1-85937-256-2	£9.99

Available from your local bookshop or from the publisher

Frith Book Co Titles (continued)

Ipswich (pb)	1-85937-424-7	£9.99	St Ives (pb)	1-85937415-8	£9.99
Ireland (pb)	1-85937-181-7	£9.99	Scotland (pb)	1-85937-182-5	£9.99
Isle of Man (pb)	1-85937-268-6	£9.99	Scottish Castles (pb)	1-85937-323-2	£9.99
Isles of Scilly	1-85937-136-1	£14.99	Sevenoaks & Tunbridge	1-85937-057-8	£12.99
Isle of Wight (pb)	1-85937-429-8	£9.99	Sheffield, South Yorks (pb)	1-85937-267-8	£9.99
Isle of Wight Living Memories	1-85937-304-6	£14.99	Shrewsbury (pb)	1-85937-325-9	£9.99
Kent (pb)	1-85937-189-2	£9.99	Shropshire (pb)	1-85937-326-7	£9.99
Kent Living Memories	1-85937-125-6	£14.99	Somerset	1-85937-153-1	£14.99
Lake District (pb)	1-85937-275-9	£9.99	South Devon Coast	1-85937-107-8	£14.99
Lancaster, Morecambe & Heysham (pb)	1-85937-233-3	£9.99	South Devon Living Memories	1-85937-168-x	£14.99
Leeds (pb)	1-85937-202-3	£9.99	South Hams	1-85937-220-1	£14.99
Leicester	1-85937-073-x	£12.99	Southampton (pb)	1-85937-427-1	£9.99
Leicestershire (pb)	1-85937-185-x	£9.99	Southport (pb)	1-85937-425-5	£9.99
Lincolnshire (pb)	1-85937-433-6	£9.99	Staffordshire	1-85937-047-0	£12.99
Liverpool & Merseyside (pb)	1-85937-234-1	£9.99	Stratford upon Avon	1-85937-098-5	£12.99
London (pb)	1-85937-183-3	£9.99	Suffolk (pb)	1-85937-221-x	£9.99
Ludlow (pb)	1-85937-176-0	£9.99	Suffolk Coast	1-85937-259-7	£14.99
Luton (pb)	1-85937-235-x	£9.99	Surrey (pb)	1-85937-240-6	£9.99
Maidstone	1-85937-056-x	£14.99	Sussex (pb)	1-85937-184-1	£9.99
Manchester (pb)	1-85937-198-1	£9.99	Swansea (pb)	1-85937-167-1	£9.99
Middlesex	1-85937-158-2	£14.99	Tees Valley & Cleveland	1-85937-211-2	£14.99
New Forest	1-85937-128-0	£14.99	Thanet (pb)	1-85937-116-7	£9.99
Newark (pb)	1-85937-366-6	£9.99	Tiverton (pb)	1-85937-178-7	£9.99
Newport, Wales (pb)	1-85937-258-9	£9.99	Torbay	1-85937-063-2	£12.99
Newquay (pb)	1-85937-421-2	£9.99	Truro	1-85937-147-7	£12.99
Norfolk (pb)	1-85937-195-7	£9.99	Victorian and Edwardian Cornwall	1-85937-252-x	£14.99
Norfolk Living Memories	1-85937-217-1	£14.99	Victorian & Edwardian Devon	1-85937-253-8	£14.99
Northamptonshire	1-85937-150-7	£14.99	Victorian & Edwardian Kent	1-85937-149-3	£14.99
Northumberland Tyne & Wear (pb)	1-85937-281-3	£9.99	Vic & Ed Maritime Album	1-85937-144-2	£17.99
North Devon Coast	1-85937-146-9	£14.99	Victorian and Edwardian Sussex	1-85937-157-4	£14.99
North Devon Living Memories	1-85937-261-9	£14.99	Victorian & Edwardian Yorkshire	1-85937-154-x	£14.99
North London	1-85937-206-6	£14.99	Victorian Seaside	1-85937-159-0	£17.99
North Wales (pb)	1-85937-298-8	£9.99	Villages of Devon (pb)	1-85937-293-7	£9.99
North Yorkshire (pb)	1-85937-236-8	£9.99	Villages of Kent (pb)	1-85937-294-5	£9.99
Norwich (pb)	1-85937-194-9	£8.99	Villages of Sussex (pb)	1-85937-295-3	£9.99
Nottingham (pb)	1-85937-324-0	£9.99	Warwickshire (pb)	1-85937-203-1	£9.99
Nottinghamshire (pb)	1-85937-187-6	£9.99	Welsh Castles (pb)	1-85937-322-4	£9.99
Oxford (pb)	1-85937-411-5	£9.99	West Midlands (pb)	1-85937-289-9	£9.99
Oxfordshire (pb)	1-85937-430-1	£9.99	West Sussex	1-85937-148-5	£14.99
Peak District (pb)	1-85937-280-5	£9.99	West Yorkshire (pb)	1-85937-201-5	£9.99
Penzance	1-85937-069-1	£12.99	Weymouth (pb)	1-85937-209-0	£9.99
Peterborough (pb)	1-85937-219-8	£9.99	Wiltshire (pb)	1-85937-277-5	£9.99
Piers	1-85937-237-6	£17.99	Wiltshire Churches (pb)	1-85937-171-x	£9.99
Plymouth	1-85937-119-1	£12.99	Wiltshire Living Memories	1-85937-245-7	£14.99
Poole & Sandbanks (pb)	1-85937-251-1	£9.99	Winchester (pb)	1-85937-428-x	£9.99
Preston (pb)	1-85937-212-0	£9.99	Windmills & Watermills	1-85937-242-2	£17.99
Reading (pb)	1-85937-238-4	£9.99	Worcester (pb)	1-85937-165-5	£9.99
Romford (pb)	1-85937-319-4	£9.99	Worcestershire	1-85937-152-3	£14.99
Salisbury (pb)	1-85937-239-2	£9.99	York (pb)	1-85937-199-x	£9.99
Scarborough (pb)	1-85937-379-8	£9.99	Yorkshire (pb)	1-85937-186-8	£9.99
St Albans (pb)	1-85937-341-0	£9.99	Yorkshire Living Memories	1-85937-166-3	£14.99

See Frith books on the internet www.francisfrith.co.uk

FRITH PRODUCTS & SERVICES

Francis Frith would doubtless be pleased to know that the pioneering publishing venture he started in 1860 still continues today. A hundred and forty years later, The Francis Frith Collection continues in the same innovative tradition and is now one of the foremost publishers of vintage photographs in the world. Some of the current activities include:

Interior Decoration

Today Frith's photographs can be seen framed and as giant wall murals in thousands of pubs, restaurants, hotels, banks, retail stores and other public buildings throughout the country. In every case they enhance the unique local atmosphere of the places they depict and provide reminders of gentler days in an increasingly busy and frenetic world.

Product Promotions

Frith products are used by many major companies to promote the sales of their own products or to reinforce their own history and heritage. Frith promotions have been used by Hovis bread, Courage beers, Scots Porage Oats, Colman's mustard, Cadbury's foods, Mellow Birds coffee, Dunhill pipe tobacco, Guinness, and Bulmer's Cider.

Genealogy and Family History

As the interest in family history and roots grows world-wide, more and more people are turning to Frith's photographs of Great Britain for images of the towns, villages and streets where their ancestors lived; and, of course, photographs of the churches and chapels where their ancestors were christened, married and buried are an essential part of every genealogy tree and family album.

Frith Products

All Frith photographs are available Framed or just as Mounted Prints and Posters (size 23 x 16 inches). These may be ordered from the address below. From time to time other products - Address Books, Calendars, Table Mats, etc - are available.

The Internet

Already twenty thousand Frith photographs can be viewed and purchased on the internet through the Frith websites and a myriad of partner sites.

For more detailed information on Frith companies and products, look at these sites:

www.francisfrith.co.uk
www.francisfrith.com
(for North American visitors)

See the complete list of Frith Books at:

www.francisfrith.co.uk

This web site is regularly updated with the latest list of publications from the Frith Book Company. If you wish to buy books relating to another part of the country that your local bookshop does not stock, you may purchase on-line.

For further information, trade, or author enquiries please contact us at the address below:
The Francis Frith Collection, Frith's Barn, Teffont, Salisbury, Wiltshire, England SP3 5QP.
Tel: +44 (0)1722 716 376 Fax: +44 (0)1722 716 881 Email: sales@francisfrith.co.uk

See Frith books on the internet www.francisfrith.co.uk

TO RECEIVE YOUR FREE MOUNTED PRINT

Mounted Print
Overall size 14 x 11 inches

Cut out this Voucher and return it with your remittance for £1.95 to cover postage and handling, to UK addresses. For overseas addresses please include £4.00 post and handling. Choose any photograph included in this book. Your SEPIA print will be A4 in size, and mounted in a cream mount with burgundy rule line, overall size 14 x 11 inches.

Order additional Mounted Prints at HALF PRICE (only £7.49 each*)

If there are further pictures you would like to order, possibly as gifts for friends and family, purchase them at half price (no additional postage and handling required).

Have your Mounted Prints framed*

For an additional £14.95 per print you can have your chosen Mounted Print framed in an elegant polished wood and gilt moulding, overall size 16 x 13 inches (no additional postage and handling required).

---

* IMPORTANT!
These special prices are only available if ordered using the original voucher on this page (no copies permitted) and at the same time as your free Mounted Print, for delivery to the same address

---

Frith Collectors' Guild

From time to time we publish a magazine of news and stories about Frith photographs and further special offers of Frith products. If you would like 12 months FREE membership, please return this form.

Send completed forms to:
**The Francis Frith Collection,
Frith's Barn, Teffont, Salisbury,
Wiltshire SP3 5QP**

Voucher for FREE and Reduced Price Frith Prints

Picture no.	Page number	Qty	Mounted @ £7.49	Framed + £14.95	Total Cost
		1	**Free of charge***	£	£
			£7.49	£	£
			£7.49	£	£
			£7.49	£	£
			£7.49	£	£
			£7.49	£	£

Please allow 28 days for delivery	*** Post & handling**	**£1.95**
Book Title	**Total Order Cost**	**£**

Please do not photocopy this voucher. Only the original is valid, so please cut it out and return it to us.

I enclose a cheque / postal order for £ . . . .
made payable to 'The Francis Frith Collection'
OR please debit my Mastercard / Visa / Switch / Amex card
(credit cards please on all overseas orders)

Number . . . .

Issue No(Switch only) . . . . .Valid from (Amex/Switch) . . . .

Expires . . . .   Signature . . . .

Name Mr/Mrs/Ms . . . .

Address . . . .

. . . .

. . . .

. . . . Postcode . . . .

Daytime Tel No . . . .   Valid to 31/12/03

The Francis Frith Collectors' Guild

Please enrol me as a member for 12 months free of charge.

Name Mr/Mrs/Ms . . . .

Address . . . .

. . . .

. . . .

. . . . Postcode . . . .

Would you like to find out more about Francis Frith?

We have recently recruited some entertaining speakers who are happy to visit local groups, clubs and societies to give an illustrated talk documenting Frith's travels and photographs. If you are a member of such a group and are interested in hosting a presentation, we would love to hear from you.

Our speakers bring with them a small selection of our local town and county books, together with sample prints. They are happy to take orders. A small proportion of the order value is donated to the group who have hosted the presentation. The talks are therefore an excellent way of fundraising for small groups and societies.

Can you help us with information about any of the Frith photographs in this book?

We are gradually compiling an historical record for each of the photographs in the Frith archive. It is always fascinating to find out the names of the people shown in the pictures, as well as insights into the shops, buildings and other features depicted.

If you recognize anyone in the photographs in this book, or if you have information not already included in the author's caption, do let us know. We would love to hear from you, and will try to publish it in future books or articles.

Our production team

Frith books are produced by a small dedicated team at offices in the converted Grade II listed 18th-century barn at Teffont near Salisbury, illustrated above. Most have worked with the Frith Collection for many years. All have in common one quality: they have a passion for the Frith Collection. The team is constantly expanding, but currently includes:

Jason Buck, John Buck, Douglas Burns, Heather Crisp, Lucy Elcock, Isobel Hall, Rob Hames, Hazel Heaton, Peter Horne, James Kinnear, Tina Leary, Hannah Marsh, Eliza Sackett, Terence Sackett, Sandra Sanger, Lewis Taylor, Shelley Tolcher, Helen Vimpany, Clive Wathen and Jenny Wathen.